BRITAIN'S HERITAGE

Holiday Trains

Greg Morse

AMBERLEY

Acknowledgements

I am indebted to Roger Badger, Derek Hotchkiss, Philip Hunt, Julia Jenkins, Gerald Riley, Debbie Stevens, Michael Woods and Nick Wright.

My thanks also go to those who supplied many of the images in this book: Colour-Rail (incorporating the work of Jack Crossley, H. N. James, the G. Parry Collection and M. H. Yardley), Getty Images, Rail Photoprints (including Alan H. Bryant ARPS, John Chalcraft, Richard Lewis, the Ray Hinton Archive and R. A. Whitfield), the Swindon Library Collection and STEAM Museum, Swindon.

Front cover: Class 50 No. 50046 *Ajax* passes the beach at Dawlish on the Devon coast with a service from Manchester to Plymouth in April 1984.

First published 2019

Amberley Publishing
The Hill, Stroud
Gloucestershire, GL5 4EP

www.amberley-books.com

Copyright © Greg Morse, 2019

The right of Greg Morse to be identified as the Author of this work has been asserted in accordance with the Copyrights, Designs and Patents Act 1988.

ISBN 978 1 4456 7921 1 (paperback)
ISBN 978 1 4456 7922 8 (ebook)

British Library Cataloguing in Publication Data.
A catalogue record for this book is available from the British Library.

Printed in the UK.

Contents

1
Introduction: Down by the Seaside

A Wiltshire summer morning and the platform's damp with rain. A line of suitcases, overcoats draped, join the buckets, spades and chattering children, as Father lights his pipe and Mum adjusts her hat. The excitement mounts, for today is Saturday and we're taking the train to Weston-super-Mare. Some will stay a week, others just a day; all will relish the sea, the air, a stroll along the Prom (where a brass band is doubtless playing something flatulent).

Had we lingered on the platform at Swindon while we awaited our holiday train, we might have been lucky enough to see the 'South Wales Pullman' pass through, as here on 10 August 1955, when No. 7018 *Drysyllwyn Castle* had charge of the Up working.

A diesel pulls in with an Up express – a sign of changing times. A tank engine nips through with a rake of vans, as a gleaming Castle puffs past her platform end admirers with a long rake of ex-Great Western stock. You board, along with the many, squeeze along the corridor and settle in an empty compartment. Not that it'll stay that way for long, of course.

Happy holidaymakers arrive at Weston-super-Mare General in this classic view. At this time, the excursion platforms at nearby Locking Road were also in use (see below).

No. 4089 *Donnington Castle* leaves Weston's Locking Road excursion station in 1959. Opened in 1914 to provide extra capacity for holiday trains, traffic downturns saw its closure in February 1967.

The porter helps a woman with her bags, as the guard checks his watch and blows his whistle. It was going to be a good day.

Setting off around 6 a.m., we'd first pass the mighty railway works, though grey ash and cinders would soon become green fields as we left Swindon's empty streets behind to thunder over Wootton Bassett Junction, and on through Chippenham to Bath and Bristol.

By the time we draw into Weston, Dad'll be dreaming of beer, Mum a wander through the Winter Gardens, your sister a dip in the open-air pool. You, of course, want to stay at the station and watch the trains coming in ... though an ice cream off the Grand Pier would be nice ...

* * * * * *

This is the classic collective memory of holiday travel by train – steam in the 1950s, crowded carriages, sandcastles, sun, pipesmoke and probably a glass or two of brown ale. The destination was Weston, but could have been Weymouth, Whitby, Swanage, Southport, Tenby, Torquay, Margate, Brighton or Blackpool.

Though railways didn't create the concept of mass holiday transit – that prize goes to the steamships that preceded them – they helped build up many of Britain's favourite seaside resorts. *Holiday Trains* plots this development, along with the rise of rambling, cycling and camping, the rise of motoring, motor coaches and foreign travel and the inevitable decline in the railway's market share. But who knew in the 1970s that by the end of the '90s it'd be possible to take a train under the English Channel and on into Paris?

The joys of Weston-super-Mare, as they were in the mid-1950s (and in some ways still are).

2
The Journey Begins

A grey morning after a light rain, and two men are making for a pocket of land with a measuring chain. Ahead of them, a party of surveyors are adjusting their spirit level. They work for a railway company. A new line is to be built, and every contour must be accurately recorded. As the pair approach, there's a shout and six or seven men in smocks appear with pitchforks. They make for the party. A young lad picks up the level and is knocked to the ground. He lies motionless. A man on horseback pounds towards the group and divides the attackers, who run this way and that, his threat to summon the magistrate ringing in their ears...

When George Eliot painted this scene in *Middlemarch*, published in serialised form from December 1871, the railways were well established, had become part of the British landscape, and had been plotted and described and celebrated by the celebrated *Bradshaw's Handbooks*. Set some forty years before, however, the book looks back at those pitchfork-wielding fools,

The Moorish Arch at Edge Hill, Liverpool, during the opening of the Liverpool & Manchester Railway on 15 September 1830. Note the luxurious state coach, in which the Duke of Wellington was to travel. No one could have known that it would soon be involved in the world's first rail passenger fatality.

who must have been lied to about the good the new technology would bring. They didn't understand. How could they understand? It was all beyond their ken. And yet they were not alone: for every thrilled and joyful Fanny Kemble there was a fearful, fretting Dionysius Lardner – an ambivalence summed up best perhaps by Turner's painting *Rain, Steam and Speed – The Great Western Railway*, which was first exhibited in the Royal Academy in 1844, and in which the train is part-monster, part-marvel as it cuts through the Berkshire landscape.

Did you know?

George Bradshaw published his first cartographic collection – *Bradshaw's Maps of Inland Navigation* – in 1833, but it would be his partnership with William Blacklock that saw him enter the world of railway timetable production. This bore fruit some six years later, by which time Britain had a network of some 1,500 route miles, stretching from London to Brighton, Bristol, Liverpool, Manchester, Newcastle, Southampton and York. In 1847, the first of the famous handbooks, *Bradshaw's Descriptive Guide to the London & South Western Railway*, duly appeared, with *Bradshaw's Continental Railway Guide* following soon after. Bradshaw himself died in 1853, but the books that bore his name would live on until 1961, before reappearing on television in the early part of the twenty-first century.

Nothing, though – not frightened farmhands, not local landowners, not the bad publicity that came when William Huskission MP was felled and killed by *Rocket* the day the Liverpool & Manchester Railway was opened in 1830 – could slow the new invention's momentum:

The famous *Rocket*, designed by George Stephenson's son Robert.

within a few weeks of opening, the world's first inter-city line was carrying its first mails; within a year, it would be taking tens of thousands to the Newton races. Similarly, within just a week of opening in 1838, the London & Southampton was putting on trains to carry 5,000 people from Nine Elms to Surbiton so they could see the Derby (as long as they didn't mind trudging 5 miles across the fields to the race course at Epsom).

It would be reduced-fare excursion trains like these that would become particularly popular, taking many not only to race meetings, but also concerts, beauty spots, and even notable cities. The zenith would undoubtedly be the 'Great Exhibition of the Works of Industry of All Nations', held at London's Hyde Park between May and October 1851, to which travel agents and independent groups arranged outings from as far afield as Yorkshire. Such was the fascination of the exhibition – with its jewellery displays, its telescopes and demonstrations – that all railways serving the capital saw considerable increases in passenger receipts; the Great Western's alone rose by over 38 per cent that year, while a certain Thomas Cook claimed to have brought 165,000 individuals into Euston.

The Great Exhibition helped open London up as a destination for tourism. The railway helped open the country up for everyone; until then, travel was expensive and time-consuming. Days out, though, were one thing; full-blown holidays were quite another…

The original Liverpool terminus of the Liverpool & Manchester Railway was here, in Crown Street. By 1833, the line had become so successful that a bigger station had to be built at the more familiar location of Lime Street.

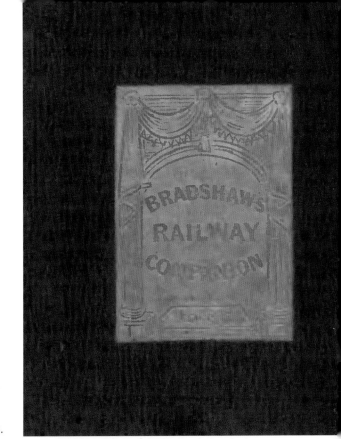

Right: The 1839 edition of *Bradshaw's Railway Companion*.
Below: The Great Exhibition of 1851 was a huge draw for visitors, which brought much business to the railway companies – and to agents like Thomas Cook. This Joseph Nash watercolour shows the exhibits put on by Jersey & Guernsey, Malta and Ceylon (Sri Lanka).

In the early nineteenth century, only the wealthy went on trips involving travel of any great magnitude. Young men (and some women) of consequence – if not substance – would take the so-called Grand Tour around Europe. Ostensibly a pilgrimage of cultural and religious import, it was essentially a rite of passage for those who could afford the passage. Back home, many were starting to make an increasing number of domestic pilgrimages by sailing ship, over 20,000 people going down to Margate thus in 1815. By 1830, steam propulsion was helping this figure to more than quadruple by fostering faster, further, and more comfortable travel. The number of resorts was on the rise too, and as they multiplied the railways woke from seeming somnambulance to meet the correspondingly growing need for transport. And when they came, prosperity followed...

Brighton is the classic case in point, having been established as a major resort in the Georgian era, the Prince Regent's patronage encouraging the great, the good and the not-so-good to attend in great numbers. The thirty-six daily stagecoaches between resort and capital carried 117,000 people in 1835. Yet when the line from resort to capital was completed six years later, the former was changed forever. Train travel was much cheaper than stagecoach travel and, while the horse-drawn held around fourteen people, the iron horse-drawn held more like 140. Trains were also much quicker – suddenly the south coast could be reached in 2½ hours. Traders were delighted, but not everyone welcomed the influx: in the words of one commentator, Brighton was veritably assailed by so many 'swarms [...] daily and weekly disgorged' from the 'cancer-like arms of the railroad'.

Gem of the southern coast was of course Brighton, represented by this postcard of the Floral Hall.

Did you know?

Thomas Cook was born in Melbourne, Derbyshire, in 1808. A wood turner by trade, he was also a strict Baptist and Temperance Society member. After moving to Market Harborough to start his own business, he organised his first excursion in 1841, hiring a Midland Counties Railway train to take 540 fellow abstainers from Leicester to a temperance rally in Loughborough. Cook would go on to arrange many more outings in the ensuing years, and – despite bankruptcy in 1846 – rallied such that he was able to take over 150,000 to the Great Exhibition, as noted in the text. This success led to his first foreign foray, which saw him arrange a trip from Leicester to the 1855 Paris Exhibition. By 1865, he'd opened a London office with his son and was working to extend his business beyond Europe. The United States was beckoning, and he sent his first tour 'across the water' in 1866.

Elsewhere, Peter Hesketh, High Sheriff of Lancashire and MP for Preston, was taking a somewhat different view, seeing that the sheltered harbour and views over Morecambe Bay gave the area around his home, Rossall Hall, the makings not only of a seaport, but also a popular resort for the less-than-affluent. With no railway between London and Scotland, he saw too its potential

The North Euston Hotel & Baths, Fleetwood-on-Wyre.

The jewel in Fleetwood's crown was the North Euston Hotel, which was built in 1841 to overlook the bay and river estuary. It was intended to serve overnight guests who had come by train from Euston, and was close to the point of departure for the steamers to Scotland. The journey was made by Queen Victoria in 1847, though the completion of the line between London and Scotland over Shap Fell rendered the town's role as a transport terminus obsolete.

ANCHOR HEAD WESTON-SUPER-MARE

The prized destination for many once the railways had come: Anchor Head, in Weston-super-Mare, c. 1909. A splendid time was guaranteed for all.

as a transfer point between trains and steamers to Scotland, and set about encouraging the laying of a line from Preston. The prominent architect Decimus Burton, admired for his work at St Leonard's-on-Sea, was engaged to plan what would become Fleetwood. Construction of the first buildings – and the line – began in 1836. Opening to the public four years later, the Preston & Wyre Railway would carry over 100,000 passengers in its first season, each vying to see the magnificent view of the Lakeland Hills and enjoy the delights of the bay.

If Fleetwood was to be the first new resort to have a line built to serve it, in 1841 Weston-super-Mare became the first established one to which a branch was built off a main line.

Weston's origins can be traced back to the Neolithic period, but it was the eighteenth-century fashion for sea bathing – sampled by George III at Weymouth in 1789 – that set it on a course away from farming and fishing. Many of the first visitors came by coach from Bath and Bristol in numbers soon sufficient to warrant a hotel, Weston's first opening in 1810.

As with Brighton, at first there were objections, local landowners being somewhat wary of this still-new technology; so much so that when Parliament granted the Bristol & Exeter Railway powers to build a line between those two cities on 19 May 1836, Brunel – the company's engineer – was obliged to bypass the town some 1½ miles to the south. As work progressed on this important broad gauge route, however, there was a change of heart (although fears about 'noisy', 'smelly' steam engines were such that when the first train arrived in the town on 14 June 1841, it was hauled by a team of horses). Equine power remained for services to and from the junction, engines being used only on through turns to Bristol.

The Great Western initially handled all operational matters, though plans for a straighter route to the West than the 'Great Way Round' led to estrangement from the chiefly Bristol-based B&E. The company started to work its own trains on 1 May 1849 and – in 1851 – began

Bulkeley, a locomotive of the 'Rover' class, which was a development of the earlier 'Iron Duke' series. Both types were capable of 80 mph and helped cement the Great Western's early reputation among holidaymakers for high-speed travel.

to use an iron horse, although the quieter four-legged variety continued to appear on evening turns until the end of March.

Brunel's original station was a small affair in Regent Street, but when the branch was doubled in 1866, a new facility was opened on the other side of the road – conveniently doing away with a decidedly inconvenient level crossing. Though modified for mixed-gauge working in 1875, it was also in this year that powers were acquired to lay a 4-mile standard-gauge loop into the town, allowing a Weston stop to be added to certain through services. By the time it opened on 1 March 1884, branches had been built to serve fourteen more seaside resorts, including Blackpool (1846), Southport (1848), Eastbourne (1849) and Torquay (1859). The railways were starting to become a key part of the nation's holidaymaking...

3

Mass Movements

There you are, an East Ender in Epping. Epping Forest to be exact. Epping Forest at Easter to be exacter still. From urban sprawl to silver birch, hustle and bustle to birdsong, you owe it all to the railway. The Great Eastern Railway to be exact...

Setting off from London's Liverpool Street, your train – hauled by a plucky 2-4-2T in its rich dark blue – had lurched over the points before passing Hackney Downs and making for the junction, where it headed north through Clapton, St James Street and Hoe Street, the view from the window growing ever more verdant until the terminus came into view: Chingford, the once rural village that was now the gateway to the forest. As you alight, your eye is caught by the dazzling smile of a local woman, but – faint-hearted – you allow yourself to be swept along with the throng of visitors who are, like you, hoping for arboreal enjoyment that day.

The Great Eastern had formed in 1862 when the Eastern Counties Railway and a number of smaller concerns had amalgamated. Its plans to build a web of lines to serve the countryside around London were soon joined by plans for a line to High Beach. The latter reached a terminus at the very end of Chingford's Hale End Road in 1873, though this small station was replaced five years later by a much larger and grander

The Great Eastern Railway's Liverpool Street station opened in 1874. By the time this photograph had been taken in 1896, it had grown to possess the largest number of platforms of any terminus in London.

BRIDGE AND STATION.

The Great Eastern didn't only run to Chingford and Epping Forest. As this image from the company's 1851 illustrated guide shows, it also ran to Norwich. Here, the station provides a backdrop to the Prince of Wales Road Bridge.

one overlooking the forest. It wasn't all that useful to the locals, but the idea was to attract tourists and stimulate suburban growth in the fields around it. Since the Bank Holiday Act of 1871, people like you could visit on Easter Monday, Whit Monday, the first Monday in August and Boxing Day, though one visitor in particular was soon to make all the difference. On 6 May 1882, Queen Victoria arrived in Chingford by train to declare the forest open to the public. 'It gives me the greatest satisfaction,' she said, 'to dedicate this beautiful forest to the use and enjoyment of my people for all time.' Thus it became 'The People's Forest', and on the day of your visit – Easter Monday 1888 – the Great Eastern would bring you and some 160,000 other passengers to one part of it or another. There were now over 13,500 miles of railway in Britain, carrying around 336.5 million passengers. Over the next forty years, there'd be 6,200 miles more, passenger numbers

Did you know?

Sadly, excursion trips were not without incident in the early days of rail travel, as the terrible accident at Armagh on 12 June 1889 demonstrated all too clearly.

In order to reach its seaside destination of Warren Point, some 24 miles away, a heavy, overcrowded Sunday School special first had to climb out of Armagh up a very steep incline. Though the rails were dry and the engine was steaming well, the heavy load proved too much and it stalled within sight of the summit at Dobbins Bridge.

The crew decided to take the first five coaches to the next station before returning for the rear ten. Unfortunately, the train was fitted with a 'simple' continuous brake, which meant that, when the vacuum pipe between the fifth and sixth vehicles was disconnected, the tail was held on the gradient by the handbrake in the guard's van alone. Some of its wheels had been scotched with stones, but when the driver eased the engine back to aid uncoupling, the ten were nudged enough to set them running back down the hill.

By this time, the next train had been dispatched from Armagh. Although its driver applied his brake when he saw the runaway heading towards him, the collision couldn't be avoided. Eighty people were killed and 260 were injured, many of them children.

GWR families wait in line at Swindon to board the trains for Trip Week, c. 1910. Destinations included Weymouth, Weston-super-Mare and Cornwall.

continuing to rise in what might justly be described as the heyday of the *Bradshaw's Handbooks* – during which the ranks of lower-middle and working-class travellers swelled. Attracting textile workers from the West Riding, Morecambe became 'Bradford-by-the-sea', Blackpool filled with Lancastrians while Tynemouth developed as a resort for the 'less wealthy' living in Newcastle.

Of course, it wasn't just the public that was enjoying the leisure possibilities the railways were providing – railway workers were as well. Take Swindon, for example. Swindon – home of Swindon Works, home of the Great Western – was also home to a Mechanics' Institution, founded 'for the purpose of disseminating useful knowledge and encouraging rational amusement amongst all classes of people employed by the GWR'. 'Useful knowledge' meant evening classes and a lending library; 'rational amusement' meant musical entertainments, theatrical entertainments and – in 1849 – an outing to the dreaming spires of Oxford. The company provided free train travel for this event, which went on to become an annual affair. In 1854, a party visited the Crystal Palace (by then relocated to Sydenham after the Great Exhibition), while the following year over 1,600 people took a 'trip' to London. And that's

Booklet of information produced for the Swindon Mechanics' Institution 'Trip' of 1912.

what the locals came to call it: 'where you goin' Trip?' would soon be a commonly posed question in the canteens, pubs, clubs and corners of the Wiltshire town.

From those humble origins, 'Trip' had grown into a nine-day break by 1874 – and its popularity was rising: in 1892, the Works closed at 1 p.m. on Thursday 7 July and didn't re-open until the morning of the 14th. By 1900, as many as 22,000 people – coppersmiths, wheelwrights, boilermakers, foremen and families – were vacating Swindon, though the peak would come in 1924, when some 29,000 were dispatched in thirty-one trains, leaving the factory – and the town – eerily silent, save for the maintenance work being undertaken during what was essentially a 'lock out' for that purpose.

Though some went to Tenby, Torquay, St Ives or Weymouth – each having a claim to the name 'Swindon-by-the-Sea' – large numbers chose Weston, with its Victorian villas, donkeys and bracing air. Weston could also be reached quickly, which made it just as viable for day trips as week-long holidays. The resort would continue to flourish, though until the law was changed in 1938, the holiday itself would be unpaid, meaning that many railwaymen went without, worked every available hour or racked up crippling debts to finance their freedom.

By the end of the nineteenth century, coastal resorts had increased in popularity and the railways were playing a major role in helping people travel to and from them. On the August Bank Holiday of 1899, seventy-six excursion trains arrived in Brighton; over the same weekend, 75,000 repaired to Ramsgate. In encouraging people to take in sea air, the railways were undeniably contributing to the health of the nation. But there were *other* 'healthy outdoor pursuits' – pursuits that didn't necessarily require the sea...

We might full imagine ourselves here too, as the sender of this postcard did: Weymouth, where many a Swindonian chose to go during Trip Week. Some still do.

The Promenade, Weymouth

4
Rambling, Camping, Cycling

Between railway mania and Beatlemania, Britain was buoyed by manias many more. One such was the noble art of cycling. By 1890, dandy horses, velocipedes and boneshakers had given way to the chain-driven 'safety bicycle', which became an obsession for increasing numbers of enthusiasts. The trouble was, the poor roads in many large towns could make these new machines feel just as shaky as the old. What you wanted – if you wanted to ride your bicycle – was the wide open countryside, a place where you could forget all your duties, all your woes, all your cares, while the wind blew through your hair and the flies got stuck in your teeth.

Step forward the railway companies, although costs were often considered high, and the precious machines were often damaged as they bounced about in the guard's van against carriage sides and cases, boxes, portmanteaux and other paraphernalia. As *Cycling* magazine explained, 'Cycles are at present placed with other luggage and it is a common occurrence for cycles to be stacked together. So little consideration for the safe carriage of cycles is shown that many are rendered unrideable by the end of the journey, and the majority are scratched or damaged in some way.'

Worse still, most railways seldom paid out for bent frames and buckled wheels. For *Cycling* (again), cyclists indeed placed themselves 'at the mercy of the railway company', and when disaster struck, it was 'an evil day for both man and machine, for verily he must have many shekels who can face the charges for the bike and the damages thereto. They give you a little

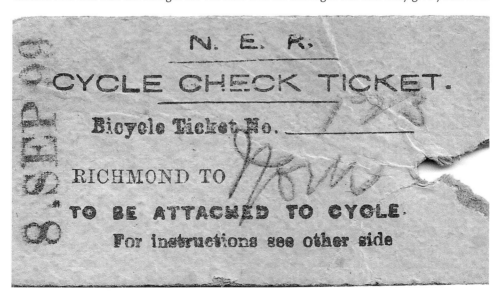

A North British Railway 'cycle check ticket', dated 8 September 1899, entitling the purchaser to convey a bicycle on a train between Richmond and York.

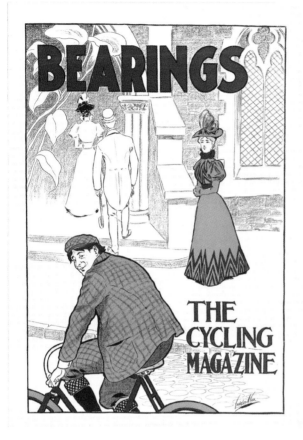

The cover of that august publication, *The Cycling Magazine*. The emphasis of this issue would seem not to be the railway, but the enthralling subject of bearings.

piece of paper, printed on the back with some infernal nonsense about "the act of God and the Queen's enemies", and this absolving themselves of any legal responsibility, proceed to pile milk-cans and packing cases on the top of the unoffending bike.' How many of the 60,000 cycles handled at Liverpool Street in the summer of 1898 so suffered? We may never know, but – unsurprisingly – it wasn't long before the railways found themselves increasingly lobbied to produce special accommodation in their trains. And so it was that the Caledonian

Did you know?

In 1799, the poet William Wordsworth and his sister Dorothy came to live at Dove Cottage in Grasmere. It was here, in this Lakeland setting, that his most famous poem, 'I Wandered Lonely as a Cloud,' would be written in 1804. A move to nearby Ambleside came in 1813 and, though he continued to write poetry, he seldom reached the heights he'd managed in earlier life.

Wordsworth was granted a government pension in 1842 and became Poet Laureate the following year. He died on 23 April 1850, his blank verse epic *The Prelude* – on which he had worked since 1798 – being published posthumously.

came to include cycle racks in the vans of the new stock for its 'Grampian Corridor' express services, which ran between Glasgow and Aberdeen from 1905.

From two wheels to no wheels... Walking – lonely as a cloud or otherwise, and as opposed to vagrancy – had been growing in popularity since the eighteenth century. Partly it was down to the romanticism, that inclination to take the Grand Tour, to which we have already alluded. Partly it was down to the Napoleonic Wars, which – from 1803 to 1815 – essentially prevented many (those pioneer Romantic Poets, Wordsworth and Coleridge, included) from travelling abroad to drink in the world's delights. For them, there was little choice but to appreciate the joys of their own landscape. The Lake District became a favourite place of pilgrimage: Thomas West, an English priest, had popularised the idea of walking there in his guide book of 1778. Just over thirty years later, William Wordsworth would be adding to the canon with his *Guide Through the District of the Lakes*. First published in 1810, its expanded 1835 fifth edition came to be revered by ramblers and academics alike.

The poet had hoped 'to give a model of the manner in which topographical descriptions ought to be executed, in order to their being either useful or intelligible, by evolving truly and

Dating from October 1915, this beautiful Furness Railway timetable cover shows the lure of Lake Windermere. Though experiencing difficulty in the 1870s, the more modern fleet of vessels on the lake by the turn of the century allowed the company to encourage (and carry) increasing numbers of day trippers and holidaymakers.

distinctly one appearance from another'. What he seems not to have realised is how appealing his descriptions would be to more than just poets. It was all that Furness Railway's fault...

The Furness was developed during the 1850s and '60s to transport coal and iron ore deposits from Lancashire and Cumberland mines to the heavy industries of north-west and north-east England. As the lines being built on the coast from Carlisle to Lancaster joined to become one, it was soon realised that the beauty Wordsworth saw could be seen by many more. In fact, as early as 1847, the Kendal & Windermere had opened a branch from Oxenholme to Birthwaite (later to become modern-day Windermere). The poet, who feared that a huge influx of people would destroy the area, and objected to the idea of becoming something of a tourist attraction himself, lamented in verse later lamented for its quality the 'mischief' that the 'long-linked Train' represented.

Yet the tide of progress was inexorable, and within three years, four passenger steamers were plying the length of the lake from Waterhead to Newby Bridge. The Furness Railway subsequently laid a line from Plumpton Junction along the River Leven, to Greenodd, but (understandably) decided to extend up the valley to meet them. The first sod was cut at Haverthwaite on 22 November 1866 by Mr James Ramsden, the Furness Railway's Managing Director (and a landowning industrialist in his own right). Construction started the following year, but the tunnelling and cutting through the area's hard rock soon put the work behind schedule. Nevertheless, another decision led to another extension – to a new terminus at Lakeside a mile further on, where larger steamers would be able to operate. To this end, shares were purchased in the Windermere United Steam Yacht Company (although this also prevented any expansion plans the Kendal & Windermere may have had, it having become part of the rival London & North Western Railway).

Ullswater, as depicted in an early twentieth-century oilette postcard – something the rambler, cyclist or camper might send to the folks back home.

The line up to Lakeside was opened with great ceremony on 1 June 1869. While its main source of revenue came from coal for the Windermere steamers, iron ore for the Backbarrow Iron Works, and sulphur and saltpetre for the Black Beck and Low Wood gunpowder works, by 1872 the 'United' vessels had been bought outright by the Furness in a bid to boost the tourist trade. Sadly, however, the iron ore industry started to decline at this time and with it went the fortunes of the company. Wordsworth – who'd long since passed – would have been delighted.

Elsewhere, trains were being used to help walkers get to somewhere worth walking more quickly. Between 1905 and 1914, the Great Western ran a special Sunday train from Paddington to five stations east of Swindon, to help speed explorations of the Vale of the White Horse. Some people – when they got to the fields around Uffington, or indeed Ulverston or Ullapool – had the bare-faced nerve to want to stay there in their own tent. This practice – 'camping' – was first popularised in Britain on the River Thames. By the 1880s, large numbers of visitors took part in the pastime, which was connected to a concurrent craze for pleasure boating. By 1894, a large commercial camping ground had opened near Douglas, on the Isle of Man. Within ten years, the Association of Cycle Campers had opened its own site in Weybridge. The early camping equipment was very heavy, so it was convenient to transport it by boat or to use craft that converted into tents. In time, the need for a tent would be dispensed with – if you wanted it to be – by the railway itself, who could rent you accommodation in a camping coach. First, though, camping would take on a very different form, as Britain prepared for battle in what would come to be called 'the war to end all wars'...

Off to a camp of a very different kind: the first contingent of the GWR Regimental Company of Railway Troops, headed by a Highland band, are seen at Paddington on 18 June 1915.

5
Between the Wars

The Britain of the early twenties was shrouded by the grey aftermath of the Great War. Many lives had been lost and many of the lives that went on would do so with indelible scars. If you read the early novels of Evelyn Waugh, you might think the country full of nought but 'Bright Young Things', who drank expensive cocktails and spoke in a strange 'mockney' dialect. But though the conflict had palpably begun to eat away at seemingly immutable class boundaries, the truth for many meant social and industrial upheaval.

Against this backdrop, the post-war coalition government tried to build the land 'fit for heroes' of which its leader, Liberal MP and former chancellor David Lloyd George, had spoken in his 1918 election campaign. Even though fate would condemn them to failure, ideological differences would rend them asunder and Lloyd George would give way to Conservative leader Andrew Bonar Law, they would manage to create a Ministry of Transport before their end came in 1922.

Nationalisation was also mooted at this stage. The railways had been sequestered into government service to ease the movement of troops and supplies during the war and had provided such sterling support that even Winston Churchill saw the advantage of running them 'at a loss to develop industries and agriculture'. State ownership in peacetime, however, proved to be a different matter. Inflation had seen the railway wage bill rise threefold between 1913 and 1920, while a coal strike the following year lost so much trade that the system was thrown some £60 million into debt.

Despite this, there remained an acceptance that the benefits of unified operation should be retained. As the first Transport Minister, Eric Geddes, put it, under 'a system of competition not only did one railway [...] strive to divert traffic from another, but trams sought to wrest traffic from the railways, railways to wrest traffic from canals [...] and so on'. 'In future,' he went on, 'our effort will be to encourage each agency of transport to undertake that part of the work which it, owing to its own special qualities, can most efficiently and economically perform.' It was a grand scheme of integration, whose first stage was embodied in the 1921 Railway Act, which came into effect on 1 January 1923, effectively amalgamating around 120 smaller companies into the famous Big Four: the Great Western, London Midland & Scottish, London & North Eastern and Southern.

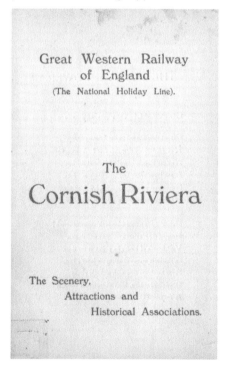

Great Western Railway
of England
(The National Holiday Line).

The

Cornish Riviera

The Scenery,
Attractions and
Historical Associations.

The Cornish Riviera, the GWR's seminal guidebook, c. 1904.

Elegant GWR 4-2-2 No. 3031 *Achilles* backs out of Paddington, *c.* 1908.

Not so much a fresh start, this was actually to be a difficult period for the industry, which would be worsened by improving road surfaces, road vehicle technology and the post-war sell-off of hundreds of ex-military lorries, which allowed private hauliers to proliferate and undercut the railway, just as the burgeoning bus and motor coach industry was doing much the same thing.

Yet trains were the still the only way to travel with speed and elegance. Could there really be any other way to reach Cromer ... Cleethorpes ... Cornwall from the capital? Certainly in 1924 there wasn't. And what *about* Cornwall? Imagine yourself preparing to make that journey. You live in Kensington. You are not without funds. Your normal holiday destination of choice is Monaco or Paris; *Bradshaw's Continental Railway Guide* sits proudly in your library. This year, though, you've been reading a guide of a different kind. This year, you're going to 'see your own country first'...

It's just after ten as your taxi pulls up in Praed Street and you open the door to the bustle of Paddington. Ducking down the slope to The Lawn, you look up at the departures board to check: the 10:30 a.m. departure, departing from Platform 1. Being so inclined, you decide to take a walk up past the Cloak Room, the Telegraph Office and the wonderfully ornate three-faceted clock to the country end of the station. There the locomotive waits while mail and milk churns are loaded into the van behind it. Simmering gently, she is a copper-capped vision in green: No. 4073 *Caerphilly Castle*, a new breed of engine powerful enough to dispense with the need for a 'pilot' to help it up and over the Devon banks.

Back on the train, you've settled in to the comfort of a First Class compartment and are just musing on the joys of luncheon when the guard's whistle blows, the engine breathes low and the train pulls out before making for Westbourne Park, West Drayton and the West.

The throng of Paddington's Platform 1 in the 1920s.

We are, of course, on the 'Cornish Riviera Express' (known to most railwaymen as the '10:30 Limited'). Through trains from Paddington to Penzance had started running on 1 March 1867 and included fast services like the 10:15 'Cornishman' and 11:45 'Flying Dutchman', but these still took 9 hours or more to make the journey. In a bid to cut the times it took to travel between London and Plymouth, the Great Western started running non-stop to Exeter, but this was only really the start and a plan soon formed for a fast train on to Penzance. Ours started life on 1 July 1904. It left London at 10:10 in those days, and was timed to reach the Cornish terminus at 5.10 in the afternoon. Originally, we'd have taken the 'Great Way Round' via Bristol, but by the summer of 1906, our train could take the new 'Berks & Hants' line through Newbury, Westbury and Castle Cary. This took the time from Paddington to Plymouth (our first stop) from 4 hours 25 minutes down to 4 hours 10. Later years would see more time shaved off as avoiding lines around Westbury and Frome opened, though it needed a new class of locomotive to take the Paddington–Plymouth timing down to 4 hours dead. These, the celebrated Kings, came in from 1927, although – at 89 tons – they were too heavy to traverse Brunel's Royal Albert Bridge over the River Tamar, meaning an engine change had to be made at the Devon port to something lighter.

The whole idea of people like Kensington-dwelling 'us' and our ilk travelling to Cornwall had been suggested, created, nurtured by the Great Western itself. A few months before

No. 4073 *Caerphilly Castle* awaits entry to Old Oak Common Carriage Sidings with empty stock from Paddington, c. 1935.

the birth of our train, the company had published a book called – enticingly – *The Cornish Riviera*, whose content was as keen as its title to link Lyonesse with its assumed Continental counterpart. On reaching Penzance, it said, if we 'walk in the Morrab Gardens, where a good band plays amongst a wealth of sub-tropical vegetation which Nice or Monte Carlo might envy,' we may, 'without any great stretch of the imagination' find ourselves 'in Algiers'. The effect was heightened by the planting of palm trees on platforms, posters which suggested Cornwall to be practically identical to Italy and the promotion of 'a land of legend and romance', in which a number of cultural pursuits could be enjoyed. Another GWR book – *Holiday Haunts* – would tell of ghosts, granite crosses, witches, smugglers, Celtic saints. It was less about sandcastles than self-improvement, and it was coming at a time when the county's traditional industries – tin mining and fishing – were starting to wane.

Of course, the Great Western wasn't the only producer of guidebooks to Cornwall (or anywhere else for that matter). Within a decade – and keen no doubt to sell as much petrol as possible – Shell began to publish a series of its own. The first (dating from 1934) covered familiar south-western ground and was written by the poet John Betjeman, better known then as an architectural journalist. Blighted perhaps by his contempt for Victorian church "restoration" (he always used double inverted commas for that word), it would be his 1964 update which agreed that 'fathers who had come for the fishing and mothers who wanted sea air for their families at cheaper rates and in less plebian conditions than those provided in Thanet or Brighton came to Cornwall'. Of course he betrays himself by telling of the building of 'monster hotels' like King Arthur's Castle at Tintagel and the Metropole at Padstow, thus reminding us that just as the GWR wasn't the only company to produce guidebooks, neither was it the only railway to reach into Cornwall. And Betjeman was a shade more on the side of its rival – the London & South Western – for that purpose, having used it as a boy.

A simply splendid group of chums 'Go Great Western' in style as their train nears the Royal Albert Bridge at Saltash in the 1930s.

The goal of 'Going Great Western': Penzance, from Newlyn Bay, as captured in oils and preserved as a postcard.

The starting point of a journey westwards with the Southern Railway was Waterloo, seen here with Urie N15 No. 754 *The Green Knight* in 1936.

SOUTHERN
The "Atlantic Coast Express"

An original 1920s postcard, showing the 'Atlantic Coast Express' in the charge of No. 850 *Lord Nelson*, the doyen of a class introduced by the Southern Railway in 1926.

By 1926, the LSWR had become part of the Southern Railway, and it was in that year that the latter launched the 'Atlantic Coast Express' – the celebrated 'ACE', which would leave Waterloo at 11:00 a.m. and power its way south-westwards. At Halwill Junction, portions for Bude and Padstow would be detached, the latter skirting the edge of Bodmin Moor before reaching Camelford, descending to Wadebridge, and following what Betjeman would later describe as the most beautiful train journey he knew, as the 'long express' passed at last so many 'minty meadows' and 'bearded trees', en route to the land of long summer holidays by the sea. North Devon was also reached via Crediton and Lapford, after which the line followed the River Taw to Barnstaple Junction, where portions for Torrington and Ilfacombe came off. Many would be taken to their final destinations by Drummond 'M7' tank engines, while the rest of the train continued behind the 'big engine' to Plymouth.

On the GWR, things were done a little differently. Not for them decoupled carriages collected by a tank engine: on the 'Cornish Riviera', a guard would pull a lever, the rearmost coach would be automatically uncoupled and – thus released – would glide effortlessly to a halt, hopefully in the station if the point of slip and the guard's control of the brake were right. Westbury would see the first 'slip coach', for passengers making for Salisbury or Weymouth, Taunton would see the next (junction for Minehead), Exeter would be the last. From here, of course, passengers could change for Paignton, Brixham or Kingswear. In the later twentieth century, the humourist and author Miles Kington would quote S. P. B. Mais' guidebook of 1929, which insisted that 'sometimes there is more likelihood of sun in Torquay as there is in Genoa'. 'Oh who'd want to be in Genoa,' asked Kington, 'when you could be in Goodrington Sands?' Who indeed? Later still, novelist Andrew Martin would refer to the title of that volume – *Glorious Devon*. And of course Devon – like Cornwall – was given that Riviera touch quite deliberately by the GWR...

This was – for some, at least – the golden age of rail travel. Pullman cars were all the rage and the Southern ran a number of luxury Pullman dining services, including several boat trains, like 'The Cunarder', which ran from London to Southampton. For *un holiday par excellence*, though, a new 'Golden Arrow'/'Flèche d'Or' service was introduced in 1929. From 15 May, trains would leave both capital cities at 11:00, that on the English side taking 98 minutes to reach Dover, where the crossing to Calais would be made aboard the Southern's new,

M7 tanks were often used to haul detached portions of the 'Atlantic Coast Express' to destinations like Ilfracombe. This example – No. 24 – is seen 'on shed' at Exmouth in 1930.

luxury, purpose-built ferry, the SS *Canterbury*.

Luxury? The Midland had long been noted for the luxury of its top-end coaching stock, but by now it was merely a big part of the biggest of the Big Four: the LMS, a sprawling monolith which brought together old rivals in an uneasy, forced marriage. The new company's early years were characterised by financial difficulty and disagreement – generally between its two largest constituents: the Midland and the London & North Western. The will of the former generally prevailed, many Midland practices being adopted as policies by the new Board. Sometimes this was beneficial, such as the decision to follow that company's centralised train control system; sometimes it was less so, as in the continuation of a 'small-engine' policy, which tended to force the widespread, and uneconomical, use of double-heading, as single locomotives could not cope with heavy loads and steep inclines. This was particularly evident on the West Coast Main Line,

Highly stylised Southern Railway poster from 1931, promoting the 6²/₃-hour 'Golden Arrow' service between London and Paris.

where punctuality had become an issue, and on the Somerset & Dorset route, where pairs of engines would struggle to haul long holiday specials up over the Mendip hills and down to Bournemouth during the summer months.

The solution began with the powerful Royal Scot class, introduced from 1927, and continued with the famous Pacific fleets built the following decade under the aegis of former Great Western man William Stanier. The year of Stanier's arrival, 1932, would also see the company reorganised to allow its commercial managers to take the lead over the operating department. Special fares (like the 'cheap day return') were thus introduced to encourage travel. Excursion traffic also increased, the company providing special trains to cater for the FA Cup Final, the Grand National and even the Blackpool Illuminations. A number of initiatives also came in to make train travel more attractive in general, including more comfortable corridor coaching stock and accelerated timings. Companies holding large freight accounts received reduced price season

The Midland/LMS 'small engine' policy in action on the Somerset & Dorset line in 1930. Here, a pair of 2P class 4-4-0s take a passenger train past Chilcompton. The route would become well known for its long holiday trains to and from Bournemouth right up until closure in March 1966.

The first move away from the old Midland 'small engine' policy came in 1927 with the launch of the 'Royal Scot' class, the first of which – No. 6100 – is seen resplendent in this period postcard.

tickets for nominated employees, while commercial travellers, pigeon fanciers and fishermen were all tempted with special offers. Unsurprisingly, passenger miles would rise from 6,500 million in 1932 to 8,500 million by 1937. The latter was also to witness the blossoming of Art Deco splendour, in the form of the 'Coronation Scot', a crack express devised to celebrate King George VI's accession. It took 6½ hours to swish passengers from Euston to Glasgow, and was hauled by the most powerful locomotive in the country: Stanier's streamlined Princess Coronation class. Finished – like the coaches – in an attractive shade of 'Caledonian Railway blue', their streamline casings were eye-catching, but fitted largely for publicity purposes, Stanier believing it to add unnecessary weight and make maintenance more difficult.

Did you know?

In 1933, the LNER adapted ten old Great Northern six-wheelers and sited them at inland beauty spots like Pateley Bridge in Yorkshire and Snettisham in Norfolk, marketing them to rail passengers as 'camping coaches'. The LMS and GWR followed suit the following year, with the Southern joining the party in 1935.

Though returning to favour after the Second World War, the number of camping coaches for hire fell from the mid-1960s as holiday preferences changed, vehicle condition deteriorated, and the number of staffed stations at which they could be sited diminished. The last were offered by BR to the public in 1971, although some continue to be available from non-railway owners.

William Stanier's tenure as LMS Chief Mechanical Engineer would not only see the 'larger engine' concept continue, but also train speeds increase. Faster trains, though, require more efficient brakes: when the LMS broke the speed record in June 1937 by reaching 114 mph with a special hauled by No. 6220 *Coronation*, disaster nearly struck when the driver failed to apply them and took the train through the 25 mph crossovers at Crewe at a heady 57.

The thrilling sight of Gresley A4 Pacific No. 2509 *Silver Link*, powering the train of the same name through Darlington.

Art Deco splendour had come to the LMS's rival for Anglo-Scottish traffic – the London & North Eastern Railway – back in 1935, with the launch of its 'Silver Jubilee' service, which had marked the twenty-fifth anniversary of King George V's reign, and which took just 4 hours to travel from Kings Cross to Newcastle at speeds of up to 100 mph (thanks largely to the A4, a new class of Pacific designed by Nigel Gresley). A booking on this train would have been ideal for the businessman in your life, but for the holidaymaker the company had introduced special 'tourist stock' – no less Art Deco, no less splendid – in a bid to increase patronage on its excursion services.

It was arguably a triumphant time for the LNER, but despite all these races to the north, races to the west, races to race meetings, seaside golf, sandcastles and sandy sandwiches, dark clouds were on the horizon. Again... For while Ethiopia had been invaded by Mussolini's Italy, Hitler had repudiated the Treaty of Versailles, sped up his rearmament programme, introduced conscription and sent his troops to the demilitarised Rhineland. When he annexed Austria, war became likely; when he invaded Poland on 1 September 1939, it became inevitable. Two days later, Prime Minister Neville Chamberlain gave his famous radio broadcast which announced to the nation that Britain was at war with Germany.

The effect on the system was almost immediate, rail being the favoured means of evacuating children and pregnant women from towns and cities considered to be at risk from bombing. Almost 1,600 trains carried 600,000 people from London during the first four days of September 1939. Many children drifted back home during the so-called 'Phoney War' – the seemingly endless period before the German Army began to advance towards Denmark and Norway. The troops transported around the same time, though, would not see home so soon. If ever. During the initial manoeuvres, some 10,000 service personnel were conveyed in twenty-two trains to the King George V dock in Glasgow for passage to the Mediterranean, where they would reinforce garrisons in Cyprus, Alexandria, Gibraltar and Malta. When conscription began in October 1939, even more were needed to move men to their billets for rapid training. Some were happy to find themselves in a seaside resort like Weston-super-Mare, spending six weeks running up and down on the beach during the day, drinking in local pubs and chatting to local girls at night. Things would soon change when they were billeted elsewhere. And for those left behind, 'See your own country first' would fast become 'Is your journey really necessary?'

An official mid-1930s photograph of a GWR camping coach interior.

Child evacuees on Maidenhead station in 1939.

6
Post-War Pleasure Trips

> It happened to be fine weather, but I expect London's stations would have been like this anyway. The vast majority of people intended to make the most of this first post-war Easter.

So said a Movietone reporter to his cinema-going audience back in April 1946. The crowds were thronging, children were longing, Mum and Dad just wanted a break. As the reporter went on, 'The people put up with the crush, and the railways coped with the people.' Yes, crushes and overcrowding and delays apart, the railways coped. Just as they'd coped during the long years of conflict, when their staff kept calm and carried on as they fought to run as regular a service as the conditions would allow. Such resolve earned rightful praise for the railways, but their efforts to get troops, military equipment and evacuees to the right place at the right time came at a price, often causing last-minute cancellations for civilian passengers, and further strain on overworked locomotives, rails and rolling stock. While some repairs were made and some new engines built for the war effort, falling revenues, and workshops given over to building tanks, shells and landing craft, meant that little more could be done.

The Great Western gets into the post-war spirit with a special 'Kiddies Express' in 1946.

Post-war steam splendour in the form of Bulleid Pacific No. 35013 *Blue Funnel*, which is seen taking 'The Devon Belle' through Basingstoke in September 1947.

A map produced by BR in 1948, showing its original six regions. These would become five from 1 January 1967, when the North Eastern was absorbed into the Eastern.

A BUTLIN CAMP THEATRE AT CLACTON

After the war, holiday camps remained as popular as ever, and many holiday journeys would have ended at one of their doors. This period postcard shows the Gaiety Theatre at Butlin's, Clacton-on-Sea.

British Railways – like its predecessor companies – liked to emphasise the historic places one could visit in Britain by train. This leaflet, which dates from the early years of nationalisation, entices the traveller to Northumbria.

When peace had come in 1945, a desire for change led to a landslide Labour victory in the subsequent general election. The Labour leader, Clement Attlee, had pledged to improve the economy, provide employment and build affordable new homes. He'd also advocated the public ownership of public services. As a result, the 1947 Transport Act heralded the nationalisation of the 'Big Four' (along with fifty smaller companies) from 1 January 1948.

Trading as 'British Railways', the system was divided into six regions (the Eastern, London Midland, North Eastern, Scottish, Southern, and Western), above which sat an executive, one of five that answered to the British Transport Commission. The latter had been established to provide 'an efficient, adequate, economical and properly integrated system of public inland transport and port facilities within Great Britain for passengers and goods'. Thus its first chairman, professional civil servant Sir Cyril Hurcomb, oversaw executives that controlled not only the railway, but also bus companies, road hauliers, docks, hotels, canals, tramways, shipping lines, London Transport, and even a film unit. And it was that unit – British Transport Films – which would help chart the development of holiday traffic over the coming twenty years or so.

Did you know?

British Transport Films was established in 1949 to make training films and travelogues exalting the virtues of places that could be reached by public transport. It also produced regular reports on progress against BR's 'Modernisation Plan'.

Led by Edgar Anstey until 1974, it worked on behalf of London Transport, British Waterways, Thomas Cook and the coach operator Thomas Tilling, although most of its output was produced on behalf of the BTC. After that organisation ceased in 1963, it made films chiefly for the British Railways Board.

In 1966, BTF won an Academy Award for *Wild Wings*, which featured Peter Scott's Wildlife and Wetland Trust at Slimbridge. It went on making films through the 1970s and early '80s, but switched off its cameras for the last time in 1982.

One of BTF's earliest efforts – 1952's *Journey into History* – echoed the emphasis of earlier advertising campaigns by encouraging viewers to travel in time as well as space. Thus, one could drop in on Roman England, Shakespeare's England, 'a hundred Englands spread through 20 centuries'. The film settles on the London of Dr Johnson, taking in the sights, sites and sounds associated with Hogarth, Gainsborough, Robert Adam and Captain Cook... It was a journey one could also take in print, many of the regional guidebooks opting to cover similar ground. The North Eastern, for example, considered Bamburgh Castle, Lindisfarne and Hadrian's Wall. Similarly, the Eastern looked at the traditional rural-historical landscape in and around Essex, the Western returned to Devon (with its white-walled cottages, 'gardens fragrant with homely flowers', 'ancient churches and gracious manor house'), while the Southern ventured to Winchester and Canterbury, as well as beautiful Broadstairs, Brighton and Bournemouth.

Many travellers wanted not these country joys, but sought the bright lights of Piccadilly and Leicester Square. Step forward *This Year – London*, which was shown to cinema audiences in 1951 and followed a staff party from a Leicester-based boot and shoe factory on their annual

Above left: By 1955, there were over 3 million cars on Britain's roads; the first section of motorway would open just three years later. This contemporary poster tries to help redress the balance, but though BR's fears about road competition would be well-founded, and though the service it offered was sometimes suboptimal, passenger receipts still rose by £2 million in 1959.

Above right: BR didn't only rely on Britain's history to entice passengers. Visit Portsmouth & Southsea in the 1950s and you could, if this poster is anything to go by, bump into Marilyn Monroe on the beach…

works trip to the Smoke. Intended to promote BR's 'party outing' service – the railway being able to arrange all travel requirements, book tickets for shows, provide packed lunches and get you home again safely – the film celebrated 'a day full of new things to see and old friends to see them with'. Arriving at St Pancras, the group make straight for the 'charabancs' awaiting them and pass Tower Bridge, the Tower of London and St Paul's as they head for lunch before taking a cruise up the river to Hampton Court ('bobbing up and down like this'), where tea is enjoyed in the Tilt Yard. There's a palpable frisson of excitement written on the faces of everyone. It was good to be alive, and they perhaps felt lucky that they were, a bomb site passed between one stop and the next reminding the viewer that the war was not long over. As if they needed reminding! Bomb sites were passed by most people every day. Bomb sites were a symbol of death that had become part of life, and there must have been much comfort in the affirmation that the Third Reich had not wiped the entire country off the planet. Hence perhaps BTF's emphasis on *The Heart of England* (1954), *The Land of Robert Burns* (1956), *The England of Elizabeth* (1957). The Baedeker Raids had been unsuccessful (though you probably didn't share that view if you were from Exeter, Bath, York or even King's Lynn).

Above: Stanier 'Black Five' No. 45147 passes the seaside town of Rhyl on the North Wales coast in October 1958.
Below: 'Black Five' No. 45052 picks up water from Moore Troughs as it heads south with a 'City of Birmingham Holiday Express', which was returning to that city from Southport on 6 August 1959.

With the famous tower rising in the background, ex-LMS Jubilee No. 45559 *British Columbia* and Stanier 3P 2-6-2T No. 40164 stand at Blackpool Central, c. 1961.

'Lynn' was the starting point for a later BTF film, featuring a (by then) well-known advocate of Britain's beauty. *John Betjeman Goes by Train* was first seen in 1962, and showed the poet and broadcaster 'leaving the London line' and heading towards the seaside town of Hunstanton. Such splendid sights are enjoyed as the long level lines lead to the grey North Sea, enjoyed by narrator and viewer alike through the windscreen of a diesel multiple unit. These beasts – and the associated replacement of steam by diesel and electric traction – had been coming since the mid-50s push for modernisation, but the fact the push didn't work, didn't stem the flow of money away from BR as hoped, meant an altogether less palatable change was now on the way. By the time Betjeman, having drunk in the delights of Wolferton and Snettisham, alights at Hunstanton and breathes in the fresh sea air, moves were afoot

Did you know?

Born in 1913, Beeching was the son of a journalist. Educated at Maidstone Grammar School, he went on to earn a first in physics at Imperial College, London, gaining his doctorate for research into electrons.

During the Second World War, he worked in armaments for the Ministry of Supply, joining ICI in 1947. The analytical mind he brought to BR came at a cost, Beeching's ICI salary of £24,000 a year being matched. This was £14,000 more than his predecessor, and £10,000 more than the Prime Minister – an absolute fortune for the time.

that would see the reduction of Britain's sprawling, nineteenth-century network to something that might turn in a profit, or at least break even.

Doctor Richard Beeching had come to the British Railways Board from ICI via a confidential committee set up by the government to find ways of cutting costs. As the BRB's new chairman, he was tasked with making the railways pay. His controversial report – *The Reshaping of British Railways* – advocated many things, but it was the long lists of service withdrawals, station closures and line closures that caught the public – and press – imagination. The report had many detractors, naturally, but one of the more legitimate criticisms was that Beeching's income figures were based on receipts issued at a specific place. This painted a gloomier picture for stations more likely to be journey's end than journey's source – not good news for seaside resorts like Lyme Regis or Robin Hood's Bay. Ironically, Hunstanton was not among those listed, though it would be closed by the close of the decade: at 9:50 p.m. on Saturday 3 May 1969, the last train for the Norfolk resort left King's Lynn. Betjeman was not among the 250-odd passengers who made the journey, nor the 250-odd waiting to greet the train, though he can't have helped lamenting the line's loss. Alas, the line's losses might have been stemmed if similar numbers had used the train more regularly. But by 1969, the British seaside had become less and less appealing to more and more British people...

The Western Region's 1961 edition of *Holiday Haunts*.

By way of contrast with our cover, the diesel era comes to Devon in the form of 'Western' class diesel-hydraulic D1041 *Western Prince*, seen here approaching Teignmouth in August 1965.

Already on borrowed time, Hunstanton plays host to a Derby lightweight DMU on 20 June 1967. Within two years, the line to the Norfolk resort will have closed forever.

7

High-Speed Holidays

A bright summer's afternoon and your clothes are almost as bright as the sun in the sky. You're at Euston. You're heading north. There are such crowds as you've never seen – but you wouldn't have: this is 25 August, this is 1967, and travelling with you are four young men who just five years ago no one had heard of. Now you're no one if you haven't heard of them. They might not have their manager in tow, but they do have Mick Jagger, Marianne Faithful, Cilla Black... and you. At least they do until you make for Second and they head for First. They are going to Bangor, to the Maharishi Mahesh Yogi, to seek spiritual enlightenment. They, of course, are The Beatles. You, of course, are not. You are heading to Llandudno to borrow your Aunt Jennifer's caravan for a week. But you're all riding on British Rail's 'high-speed' flagship: the newly electrified West Coast Main Line.

Despite the government's various attempts to cut costs, a full timetable of electric services had begun between the capital, Manchester and Liverpool Lime Street on 18 April 1966. Such were the hopes for increases in passenger numbers that BR asked well-known railway author O. S. Nock to write a book. Published later that year, *Britain's New Railway* delighted in the fact that, at one time, 'a journey between London and Liverpool, or London and Manchester,

AL3 E3033 arrives at Euston in April 1967 with a rake of coaches in BR's (then) new corporate livery. The blocks of flats in the background are a reminder that it wasn't just the railway that modernised in the 1950s and '60s.

➤ Your New Railway

LONDON MIDLAND ELECTRIFICATION

April 1966

Two shillings and sixpence

The cover of *Your New Railway*, a special booklet produced by British Rail to mark the start of public electric-hauled InterCity services from Euston in 1966.

would have been considered as "long-distance" travel; but in this era, when cities such as Zurich or Rome are within two hours' flying time to London airport the new railway services have been geared to the tempo of this modern age.' And it was a modern age, this white-heat-of-technology-age, where suddenly all the disruptions suffered while the wires were going up seemed worthwhile.

Did you know?

While railways – almost since their inception – had been able to convey horse-drawn carriages on open wagons, and later motor-cars in special trains, the first long-distance car-carrying service per se – between King's Cross and Perth – was launched in 1955. Eleven years later, the – by now expanded – service was re-branded 'Motorail' and a new, specially designed terminal opened at Kensington Olympia, the first of its kind in the world. Popular initially, the service was carrying 100,000 a year at its peak in the early '70s to places like St Austell, Stirling, and Fishguard, though traffic ebbed as increasing numbers of people took foreign holidays. Services were drastically reduced for the 1982 season, but ceased altogether in 1995 as British Rail was being privatised. The private operator of sleeper services from Paddington to Penzance reintroduced them in 1999, but they proved unprofitable and had gone again by the end of 2005.

June 1967 was part of the Summer of Love, but it was also on the cusp of the change from steam to diesel and electric traction on the Southern, as exemplified by this contemporary view of Bournemouth, where electro-diesel E6041 is in the company of a Bulleid Pacific. Steam finally left the Waterloo–Weymouth route the following month.

By this time, though, car ownership was on its way to ten million, the motorway network was starting to expand and the lure of foreign travel was becoming a real possibility for many. By this time too, Beeching had been replaced by long-term public servant Stanley Raymond, who refused to accept defeat in the face of road and air competition, who was keen to refine BR's marketing strategy, and who fought to build a nationwide 'brand' with a clear identity. Thus in 1966, 'Motorail' became the new name of BR's car-carrying passenger service and 'Inter-City' became synonymous with comfortable, crack expresses like yours.

Motorail

More and more motorists are making use of the motorail way to take their cars and families on holiday, without the exhaustion of travelling to and from holiday areas on congested roads. The Motorail network will be developed on selected routes in the 1970s with overnight sleeping accommodation on longer journeys. British Rail pioneered this car-by-train service which is now also operating on continental railways. Motorail users have doubled in the past four years and the service features strongly in the emerging pattern of fast and comfortable passenger travel.

BR brochure, detailing plans for its 'Motorail' car-carrying service, which already allowed motorists to take their cars on journeys from Swansea to Perth, Stirling to Totnes, or to Holyhead (for Ireland) and Newhaven (for France).

BTF was, of course, soon on the case, telling the British population that trains were *The Good Way to Travel* (1966) before urging British motorists to *Give Your Car a Holiday* (1967). The latter emphasised stress-free freedom, for once the BR man had put your precious Austin, Morris or Wolseley on the special flatbed wagon you were free – free to sit back and let someone else do the driving, free to have a snack, read the paper, drink in the delights of the countryside as it swished by (a novelty for any motorist). As narrator Raymond Baxter (the BBC's motoring correspondent) explained, from Liverpool you could drive to Newton-le-Willows for a train around seven in the morning and be in Torbay by two. But if you used one of the many services to one of the many ports, you could go so much further... 'A maritime nation, the British. And proud of it,' says Baxter, pointing out how you could also travel from Stirling to the South of France 'with less than a mile on the clock'. Yes! Motorail was the key to the Continent – Dunkerque could 'save you hours to Belgium, Holland and Germany', Dieppe 'saves road miles to Paris', while the routes from Newhaven could also take you to Spain or Portugal. Ireland was easily accessible, as were the Scottish Islands from places like Wemyss Bay and Gourock.

By 1969, BTF was trying again, filming a journey from Kensington Olympia to Newton Abbot, where members of the London Motor Club were set to compete with their Devonian counterparts for a specially conceived 'Motorail Trophy'. By 1969, BR had entered into an agreement with Godfrey Davis to provide car-hire facilities at major stations. It was all part of its fight against the car, the road coach and aeroplane. But the Board knew the war was far from won. In the July of that year, the next salvo came in the form of a design exhibition at the Haymarket....

Amid the displays of innovation and invention in its hotels, stations and sleeper services was a full-size mock-up of a new carriage interior and an extraordinary model of a new train. BR claimed it would help make the 1970s 'a decade of progress such as railways have never seen'.

the next train...

This brochure set out BR's plans for passenger travel in the 1970s. In addition to the striking APT imagery, it also advertised the company's station, catering, hotel and sleeper service refurbishments, along with its many other facilities.

Golden
Rail 1972
Happy-go-easy holidays
by British Rail

Packaged holidays in
BLACKPOOL

A glorious Golden Rail brochure from 1972, enticing readers to be Blackpool-bound.

A Golden Rail holiday did not have to involve a BR-owned hotel, though through British Transport Hotels, it did run several, including the Charing Cross and – as seen here – the Gleneagles, whose 700-acre Perthshire site featured two championship golf courses.

Market research had found that, with journey times of up to 3 hours, rail was the mode of choice and had the added advantage of delivering travellers close to shops and office blocks. Beyond 3 hours, people tended to let the plane take the strain. Electrification, though clearly a solution, was expensive, and while the £55 million project to raise the wires right through to Glasgow would be approved in February 1970, it had become clear that – if rail were truly to compete with air – a new train would be needed.

It was understood that anything faster than 125 mph would need a total rethink in terms of track alignment and signalling. The famous Japanese 'bullet trains' were operating at speeds of up to 130 mph on purpose-built lines with gentle gradients and few curves, but a group of ex-aerospace engineers at BR's Research Division wondered whether faster trains could be run on existing infrastructure by improving rolling stock suspension. From this idea came the Advanced Passenger Train – the APT – which could attain speeds of up to 155 mph, minimising passenger discomfort by tilting into curves. The project had secured partial government funding in 1968 and now had clearance to construct a four-car experimental train, 14-mile test track and laboratory.

Watching from the sidelines were the traditional railway engineers, many of whom were less than impressed with these aerospace 'upstarts'. They felt sure an alternative was possible, and had soon sketched out rough plans for a 'High Speed Diesel Train' (HSDT), which could reach the magic 125. By the autumn of 1970, £800,000 had been granted for the development of a prototype.

In time, the APT would fail; in time, the production 'HST' would revolutionise rail travel, creating a world where Bristol was a mere 70 minutes from London, and where passengers could enjoy a 'Great British Breakfast' as their train terrified rabbits from their line-side resting place. HSTs would also allow commuters to live further away from their London offices … just as long as they lived in Reading, or Swindon, or Peterborough…

BR's High Speed Trains revolutionised rail travel in Britain, for commuters … and holidaymakers, as the network spread beyond the original Great Western Main Line. Here, No. 253034 approaches Dawlish with the 14:47 Penzance–Paddington on 16 August 1980.

MERRYMAKER

Ideas for days out by train

From Swansea, Neath, Port Talbot, Bridgend, Cardiff and Valleys, Barry, Newport, Hereford, West & Heart of Wales

12 May to 5 October 1980

A 'Merrymaker' leaflet from 1980.

But though it was possible to swish one's way to Weston-super-Mare, and though BTF encouraged overseas tourists to buy BritRails passes and use the fast, exciting new trains, they were (at least at the beginning) only seven coaches long, and – despite the growing popularity of Torremolinos, Watneys Red Barrel, calamari and chips, sun tan oil and sangria – most 'excursions' still required something longer. Not that they were called 'excursions' any more: in 1971, BR redubbed them 'Merrymakers', and in a much longer train of much older carriages, one could use them to get to the Lakes, Llandudno, Torbay, Rhyl, Ryde, Skegness, Weymouth, almost anywhere we've met on our journey so far, cheaply. And you didn't have to change!

In that first year, fifty-five trains carried 22,000 passengers in the London division alone. Enthusiasts loved them as much as holidaymaking families, as they allowed unmarked pages of the ABC to be visited perhaps for the first time. Those from the South and West could marvel at the electric locomotives of the Midlands – all roads led to Birmingham New Street; those from the north could tick off a few of those strange Western Region diesel-hydraulics and everyone heading to the historic city of York eschewed the Shambles and the Minster for the thrum of a Deltic as it growled through the station.

Thanks to the HST, though, the Deltics and diesel-hydraulics were on borrowed time. So too – in effect – were the Merrymakers, and the

Did you know?

As well as the Merrymakers, BR also launched 'Golden Rail' in 1971. The idea was to marry train bookings with accommodation bookings. Within two years, breaks by rail were being offered to thirty-three resorts. By 1975, the list had increased by ten to include Ayr, Fort William and the Lake District. By 1980, 139,000 holidaymakers went 'Golden Rail'. Like so much outside BR's 'core business' of running trains, though, government pressure led to the brand being sold off in 1989.

merry-making they were trying to support (or create). What a pity it was there was no way to catch a train to foreign climes – not via a train ferry, but properly, like one would from London to Edinburgh, Swindon to Swansea, Crewe to Colwyn Bay ... a Merrymaker for the Continent, in fact...

Above: Class 50 No. 50007 *Hercules* takes a St Austell–Paddington 'Motorail' service through Berkley (near Frome) on 29 August 1981.

Below: Throughout the 1970s and '80s, British Rail ran special trains to Skegness using pairs of Class 20s. These ostensibly freight-only locomotives ensured the services a loyal following among enthusiasts as well as holidaymakers. In this view, Nos 20160 and 20180 pass Sleaford on 14 August 1983 en route to the resort with a train from Leicester.

GATWICK EXPRESS

CATCH THE TRAIN AND YOU'VE CAUGHT THE PLANE

GATWICK EXPRESS

10 May to 31 December 1987

In a bid to tap into the holiday flight market, BR launched special 'Gatwick Express' services linking the airport with London Victoria. This leaflet dates from 1987, two years after the reallocation from Network SouthEast to InterCity, which also saw the original slogan and neat variation on the standard BR logo 'change hands'.

8

Gateway to the Continent

So we're off at last! A long weekend in Paris: the Arc de Triomphe, the Champs-Élysées, Notre Dame... Once upon a time, we'd have flown or maybe got the ferry. Now we can check in at St Pancras, put our feet up till the call comes, and then take our place in a plush seat on a Eurostar, which will swish us all the way from Thames to Seine at speed.

The Channel Tunnel was a Victorian idea supported by BR in the '70s, cancelled by Whitehall, and finally ratified by the British and French governments in 1986. As that decade

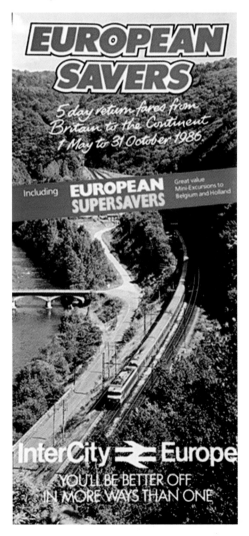

In the pre-Channel Tunnel 1980s, BR advertised the many connections that could be made between its own InterCity services and those in mainland Europe.

drew to a close, work would be well under way on *le project magnifique*, which was officially opened on 6 May 1994 by the Queen and French president François Mitterand. Back then, the British terminal for this traffic was Waterloo, but the route to the tunnel was slow; by the end of 2007 it had been replaced by a faster one into the old Midland Railway masterpiece, which was given a facelift at the buffer stop end and a shoe box at the other for domestic services. Ah well, Betjeman – whose statue gazes up at Barlow's great train shed – would have been half impressed...

Of course, we needn't go to Paris: Brussels is easily reached, so (at last) is Amsterdam. And if we go to the 'shoe box' we can get ourselves to Sheffield or Leeds, either to explore Britain's old industrial heartlands or change for seaside destinations in the north. Not only that, we can take that modern-day Motorail, Le Shuttle, load up our car at Folkestone, sit back, glide off again near Calais and make for a gîte in Calvedos or Clermont-Ferrand. Where Great Aunt Gertie marvelled at the Blackpool Tower, we can ogle the La Tour Eiffel, and swap St Michael's Mount for Mont Saint-Michel. Le café culture de la Continent is ours for le taking. Mange tout!

It's all a long way from that golden memory of the fifties railway, of steam, of sandcastles, sun, pipesmoke and brown ale. The pipesmoke – any sort of smoke – has long been banished, brown ale is harder to come by, but the destinations can still be reached. Well, some of them.

Brand-new 'Eurostar' electric-multiple units stand at Waterloo International in May 1995.

Homecoming holidaymakers get ready to replace their outgoing counterparts as No. 332005 arrives at Heathrow Terminal 4 with a 'Heathrow Express' service from Paddington. These trains had been a joint initiative between BR and BAA, though the latter took over completely before the privatisation of the former began in 1994.

We can journey to Weston, to Weymouth, Whitby, Tenby, Torquay, Margate, Brighton and Blackpool, for sure. Swanage, though, is a bit trickier.

Like Hunstanton, Swanage wasn't listed in the (in)famous Beeching Report, but a review of unprofitable branch lines led BR to announce that it would be closed by September 1968. Problems of summertime bus provision saw a reprieve, but at last the end came, the final train leaving the Isle of Purbeck on 3 January 1972. Just a decade before, the goods yard at the station would have been filled with carriages in the summer months; now it was naught but a single line into a single platform. A shadow.

By the time the Eurostars arrive à Paris, though, a preservation society will have reopened the line as far as Corfe Castle, allowing passengers to relive days they'd never lived through, or had all but forgotten. By the time St Pancras had replaced Waterloo, the Dorset holidaymaker could press on to a park and ride at la Gare du Norden. In the future lay a link remade with the main line. In the future lay a link from Swanage all the way to Paris... Brussels... Amsterdam... Berlin...

Steam splendour on the preserved Swanage Railway in the form of S15 No. 828 and Standard Class 4 No. 80104, captured as they pass New Barn on a gala day in September 2002.

9
What Now?

Reading and Viewing

This book is intended to be a summary of the development of British holiday rail travel and is not, therefore, an exhaustive survey. More detailed general information may be found in the following volumes:

Austin, Chris, and Richard Faulkner, *Holding the Line: How Britain's Railways Were Saved.* (Oxford Publishing Co., 2012). An in-depth study of railway closures, including the Beeching era and its aftermath.

Burdett Wilson, Roger, *Go Great Western: A History of GWR Publicity* (Atlantic, 1987).

Bradshaw, George, *Bradshaw's Handbook 1863* (Old House, 2012).

Bunce, Charlie, *Great British Railway Journeys* (Collins, 2011).

Cole, Beverley, and Richard Durack, *Railway Posters 1923–1947* (Laurence King, 1992).

Holland, Julian, *Railway Day Trips: 160 Classic Train Journeys Around Britain* (Collins, 2017).

Hylton, Stuart, *The British Seaside: An Illustrated History* (Amberley, 2018).

Thomas, David St John, and Simon Rocksborough Smith, *Summer Saturdays in the West* (David & Charles, 1973).

Wolmar, Christian, *Fire and Steam: A New History of the Railways in Britain* (Atlantic Books, 2007).

The British Film Institute has released a number of British Transport Films' finest documentaries on DVD, including those mentioned in this book, like *Journey into History* and *John Betjeman Goes by Train*. They are available from a variety of online and high street stores.

Web Resources

The National Archives: www.nationalarchives.gov.uk. The National Archives – formerly the Public Record Office – has an online catalogue, listing its collection of official and business-related documents. Copies of some items may be ordered through the site. Visits may also be arranged.

The Railways Archive: www.railwaysarchive.co.uk. Most of the source documents referred to in this book may be downloaded free-of-charge from this important online resource.

RailServe: www.railserve.com. This is a comprehensive guide to 19,000 railway websites and upcoming events. It features 180 categories, spanning railway travel, railway enthusiasm, and the railway industry.

Search Engine: www.nrm.org.uk/researchandarchive. The National Railway Museum has an extensive online library and archive. Catalogues list details of the museum's extensive collection of papers, drawings, reports, timetables, photographs and so on. Copies of many items can be ordered through the site.

Places to Visit

Museums

Barrow Hill Roundhouse Railway Centre, Campbell Drive, Barrow Hill, Chesterfield, Derbyshire, S43 2PR. Telephone: 01246 472450. Website: www.barrowhill.org.

Crewe Heritage Centre, Vernon Way, Crewe, Cheshire, CW1 2DB. Telephone 01270 212130. Website: www.crewheritagecentre.co.uk.

National Railway Museum, Leeman Road, York YO26 6XJ. Telephone: 01926 621261. Website: www.nrm.org.uk.

'Locomotion', the National Railway Museum at Shildon, Shildon, County Durham, DL4 1PQ. Telephone: 01388 777999. Website: www.nrm.org.uk/PlanaVisit/VisitShildon.aspx.

STEAM: the Museum of the Great Western Railway. Fire Fly Avenue, Kemble Drive, Swindon, Wiltshire SN2 2EY. Telephone: 01793 466646. Website: www.steam-museum.org.uk. Relive the glory days of the Cornish and Devon Rivieras...

Heritage Railways

Bo'ness & Kinneil Railway, The Scottish Railway Preservation Society, Bo'ness Station, Union Street, Bo'ness, West Lothian EH51 9AQ. Telephone: 01506 822298. Website: www.srps.org.uk/railway. A 10-mile line through the beautiful Scottish countryside.

Dartmouth Steam Railway & Riverboat Co. Queen's Park Station, Paignton, Devon TQ4 6AF. Telephone: 01803 555872. Website: www.dartmouthrailriver.co.uk. 7-mile standard gauge line between Paignton and Kingswear, via Goodrington Sands. Also operates ferry from Kingswear to Dartmouth.

East Somerset Railway, Cranmore Station, Shepton Mallet, Somerset BA4 4QOP. Telephone: 01749 880417. Website: www.eastsomersetrailway.com. Ideal day out from Weston-super-Mare.

Lakeside & Haverthwaite Railway, Haverthwaite Station, Nr Ulverston, Cumbria LA12 8AL. Telephone: 01539 531594. Website: www.lakesiderailway.co.uk. See the land that inspired Wordsworth.

Llangollen Railway, The Station, Abbey Road, Llangollen, Denbighshire LL20 8SN. Telephone: 01978 860979. Website: www.llangollen-railway.co.uk.

North Norfolk Railway, Sheringham Station, Station Approach, Norfolk NR26 8RA. Telephone: 01263 820800. Website: www.nnrailway.co.uk.

North Yorkshire Moors Railway, 12 Park Street, Pickering, North Yorkshire YO18 7AJ. Telephone: 01751 472508. Website: www.nymr.co.uk. Includes services through to Whitby.

Swanage Railway, Station House, Railway Station Approach, Swanage, Dorset BH19 1HB. Telephone: 01929 425 800. Website: www.swanagerailway.co.uk. Reconnected to the main line network, this line's principal terminus lies in the middle of a classic seaside town.

Wensleydale Railway, Leeming Bar Station, Leases Road, Leeming Bar, Northallerton, North Yorkshire DL7 9AR. Telephone: 01677 425805. Website: www.wensleydalerail.com. 16-mile run through the magnificent Yorkshire Dales.

West Somerset Railway, The Railway Station, Minehead, Somerset TA24 5BG. Telephone: 01643 704996. Website: www.west-somerset-railway.co.uk. 26-mile heritage line through the Quantocks to the Somerset resort.

Many holiday destinations, like Weston, Weymouth, Southend, Tenby, Torquay, Margate, Brighton and Blackpool, remain on the national network. For details of train services, readers are recommended (in the absence of Bradshaw) to try www.nationalrail.co.uk. For those venturing through the Channel Tunnel, www.eurostar.com and www.eurotunnel.com will be useful.

Getting Involved

There are many railway societies, model railway societies and preservation societies in Britain. Here is just a small selection of some of the more general ones:

The Electric Society (www.electric-rly-society.org.uk) caters specifically for those interested in electrified railways across the world. It holds regular meetings in London and Birmingham.

The Historical Model Railway Society (www.hmrs.org.uk) was founded in 1950 by historians and modellers to collect and exchange records, drawings and photographs in the interests of historical accuracy in modelling. With around 2,000 members worldwide, it remains strongly committed to gathering and distributing UK railway information. It has a large collection of photographs and drawings, a large library and has published a series of definitive books, largely concentrating on railway liveries.

The Railway Correspondence and Travel Society (www.rcts.org.uk) caters for people interested in all aspects of railways past, present and future. It publishes a monthly magazine – *The Railway Observer* – organises local meetings, has a lending library open to members and produces books of enviable accuracy.

The Signalling Record Society (www.s-r-s.org.uk) maintains and shares knowledge of railway signalling and operation in Britain and overseas. It publishes books and possesses much archive material, including photographs and drawings which may be purchased. Modern material is being added to the digital archive regularly. Members are able to download some of the digital material free-of-charge.

Experiences and Volunteering

Heritage railways are only really possible because of the huge volunteer workforce that helps keep them running. From cooks to cleaners, drivers to guards, signal staff to station masters, most will be giving up their spare time to work gratis in an environment they love. If you are keen to join in, it is best to contact your chosen heritage line direct. For non-safety related roles, basic training will probably be provided, but anything involving the movement of trains is likely to require more rigorous preparation, testing of one's understanding of operating rules and so on.

If, however, the experience of driving a train is sought on a more informal basis, many short courses are available that allow members of the public to drive a steam or diesel locomotive. Again, contacting individual heritage lines direct (via their websites) is the most effective way to find the right course for you.

Collecting

Railways were veritably made for collecting, from large items like locomotive nameplates – some of which can run to thousands of pounds – to smaller pieces like clocks or watches. For the larger ephemera, specialist auction houses (like Great Central Railwayana Auctions – www.gcrauctions.com) are recommended, though you can start a collection of tickets, timetables or postcards, say, by visiting car boot sales, model railway exhibitions or any online auction site. Many railway enthusiast magazines include features on recent sales and high-value items of interest.